VINCENT DELIEUVIN OLIVIER TALLEC

WHAT'S SO SPECIAL ABOUT
MONA LISA ?

English translation by David Michaelson and Jonathan Michaelson

ACTES SUD junior

LOUVRE
éditions

SUMMARY

La Gioconda at the Louvre Museum

La Gioconda, which is also called the *Mona Lisa*, is the most famous painting in the world. Each year, millions of visitors throng to see the painting in one of the Louvre Museum's largest exhibition rooms. Her name and image have been reproduced on every continent on coffee cups and T-shirts, in adverts and films, on the Internet, and on the facades of restaurants and beauty salons. Wherever we are and whatever we are doing—whether we are on a street corner, opening a magazine, or turning on the television—, *La Gioconda*'s smile is omnipresent.

But why do people find *La Gioconda* so fascinating?

There is something mysterious about the *Mona Lisa*. Newspaper articles and television programmes regularly announce a new discovery that will finally reveal her secret and explain her famous smile, or why her gaze follows the viewer.

But first, who is *La Gioconda*?

1.

WHO IS *LA GIOCONDA?*

Leonardo da Vinci, *La Gioconda*, c.1503–1519, Louvre Museum, Paris

LEONARDO DA VINCI'S MASTERPIECE

Leonardo da Vinci, one of the greatest artists of the Renaissance, was born in 1452 in Vinci, near Florence. It was in this town, which was the artistic capital of Italy, that he learnt to paint and where, between 1500 and 1503, he decided to begin work on a painting that quickly became famous and was called *La Gioconda*. The painting represents a young lady seated in a room in a palace, opening onto a vast landscape. This type of composition, which focuses on a person, is known as a portrait. But who is this young lady who is smiling at us?

THE PERSON IS INDEED A WOMAN

Leonardo painted *La Gioconda* over five hundred years ago and, unfortunately, there is no mention of the work in his notebooks. It was therefore necessary to carry out an investigation to identify the woman. There is still some disagreement about the person's identity. Some even believe that the person is a man.

Leonardo da Vinci, *Self-Portrait*,
c.1513–1517, Royal Library, Turin

However, in Leonardo's time, men were never represented with woman's hair and clothing. So this theory does not really hold ground. Do not believe, as is sometimes said, that it is a portrait of one of Leonardo's pupils, or even a self-portrait. Leonardo was extremely handsome, but the only known portrait of him represents him as an old man, around the same time he painted *La Gioconda*. In addition, it bears no resemblance to the *Mona Lisa*.

La Gioconda—and there is absolutely no doubt about this—is indeed a woman. But who exactly is she?

SIGNORA GIOCONDA

Thanks to a certain Giorgio Vasari, one of the first art historians, it is possible to understand why the painting was given the title *La Gioconda*. In 1550, Vasari wrote a large book entitled *Lives of the Most Excellent Painters, Sculptors, and Architects*. In the book, he wrote an account of the life of Leonardo da Vinci and the story behind *La Gioconda*.

This is his account: 'Leonardo undertook to execute, for Francesco del Giocondo, the portrait of his wife Mona Lisa, and after he had lingered over it for four years, he left it unfinished [...]. Mona Lisa being very beautiful, while he was painting her portrait, he retained those who played and sang, and continually jested, who would make her to remain merry, in order to take away that melancholy

Cesare Maccari, *Leonardo da Vinci painting the Mona Lisa*, 1863, Superintendancy, Siena

which painters are often wont to give to their portraits. And in this work of Leonardo there was a smile so pleasing, more divine than human to behold, so marvellous that she appears to be alive.'

La Gioconda does, in fact, represent the wife of Francesco del Giocondo. Leonardo used the feminine form of her surname, 'Gioconda', and it was then translated into French as 'Joconde'. La Gioconda is therefore quite simply the portrait of Signora (Mrs) Gioconda.

LA GIOCONDA

Leonardo very probably began to use this title for his painting. It should be noted that in Italy, it is possible to refer to a wo-man without saying 'Signora': there was therefore no need to use the term 'Signora Gioconda'—'La Gioconda' sufficed. It was understood that the term referred to the wife of 'Signor Giocondo'. This would not have been possible in France: it is very impolite to refer to a woman in that way.

Over time, the painting continued to be called La Gioconda. The proof: one of Leonardo's best pupils, nicknamed Salai, produced a copy of the Mona Lisa, which was also called La Gioconda. It was only in 1525, six years after Leonardo's death, that the title La Gioconda was officially used for the first time. One hundred years later, in 1625, a certain Cassiano dal Pozzo, a great connoisseur of Italian art, discovered Leonardo's painting, which he found impressive. But because he did not know the identity of the woman represented, he just called it 'a certain Gioconda', without realising that it was Lisa del Giocondo.

MONA LISA OR GIOCONDA?

Leonardo's title is still used to refer to the painting: *La Gioconda* in Italy and *La Joconde* in France. But in England and the United States, the sitter's forename is generally used: *Mona Lisa*. 'Mona' is, in fact, short for the Italian word 'Madonna', which means 'My Lady'. 'Mona Lisa' therefore means 'Madame Lisa' or, in its abbreviated form, 'Lady Lisa'. Lady Lisa or Gioconda ... you can choose the name you prefer!

MONA LISA'S LIFE

Fortunately, something is known about Mona Lisa's life. She was born in Florence on 15 June 1479. Her family, the Gherardini, was a noble family that possessed lands in Tuscany. Her parents did not work and lived off the rent from this land. Their daughter's marriage to Francesco del Giocondo was highly advantageous for them: it brought them a certain amount of wealth.

Francesco del Giocondo belonged to a rich bourgeois family, which had made its money in the silk trade. He was born in Florence on 19 March 1465 and was therefore fourteen years older than Lisa. They married in 1495. Lisa Gherardini was henceforth known by her husband's name and was called 'Mona Lisa del Giocondo'. They soon had children: Piero in 1496, Camilla in 1499, Andrea in 1502, Giocondo in 1507, and lastly, Marietta. They lived in Florence—in the Via della Stuffa, a road that still exists today.

Unfortunately, very little else is known about her. However, it is said that she was very beautiful, perhaps because she bought snail slime-based products. Was it a beauty cream or medicine? To tell the truth, we just do not know.

After Francesco's death in 1539, Lisa lived with her daughter, who was a nun in the Sant'Orsola convent, which was next to her house. She died there on 15 July 1542 and was buried there.

THE PORTRAIT OF LISA

Leonardo began working on the portrait of Lisa around 1503. This is known thanks to a certain Agostino Vespucci, who saw the painting in its initial stages in Leonardo's studio in October 1503, and mentioned it in one of his books. Lisa was then twenty-four years old.

During this period, people frequently commissioned artists to paint their portrait or that of a family member. Photography had not been invented yet, so this was the only way to create a lasting image of a person's face.

Francesco del Giocondo probably asked Leonardo to paint his wife's portrait. In 1503, she had recently given birth to her third child. The family had grown and Francesco had bought a new house that was next door. Francesco may have commissioned his wife's portrait to celebrate this happy event.

It was not easy to have a portrait painted by Leonardo, who was already one of the most famous artists in the world. At the time, all the great princes wanted a painting by him. The Duchess of Mantua, Isabella d'Este, also asked him to paint her portrait. But Leonardo chose to begin work on Lisa's portrait. Why? Probably because he knew Francesco del Giocondo. Perhaps they were close friends. Leonardo may also have been fascinated by Lisa's face or personality ...

THE *MONA LISA* WAS NEVER COMPLETED

The completed portrait was, of course, intended to be hung in Francesco and Lisa's house. But Leonardo painted very slowly. It has to be said that he was very busy with various other activities. Not only did he travel extensively, but he also studied mathematics, geometry, anatomy, the flight of birds, and many other subjects that interested him.

Leonardo also began work on other paintings such as *Saint Anne* and *Saint John the Baptist*, which are now in the Louvre Museum. It is therefore likely that he only worked on his *Mona Lisa* from time to time. And that is why he kept the painting until the end of his life! In 1506, he left Florence and went to Milan; he then went to Rome and eventually arrived in France in 1516. He took the painting with him wherever he went, even to his last home, the small Château of Cloux, near Amboise. The Cardinal of Aragon, the grandson of the King of Naples, saw the painting in the chateau when he paid a visit to Leonardo accompanied by his entire retinue, in 1517.

Leonardo da Vinci, *Saint John the Baptist*, c.1508–1519, Louvre Museum, Paris

Leonardo da Vinci, *The Virgin and Child with Saint Anne*, known as *Saint Anne*, c.1503–1519, Louvre Museum, Paris

Here is an account of the event: 'Monsignor and the rest of us went to see, in one of the outlying parts of Amboise, Messer Leonardo da Vinci the Florentine, an old man of more than seventy years, the most excellent painter of our time, who showed his Eminence three pictures, one of a certain Florentine lady, painted in a natural manner at the instance of Guiliano de' Medici [sic], another of Saint John the Baptist as a youth, and one of the Madonna and Child in the lap of Saint Anne, all most perfect.'

WILL IT BE FINISHED SOON?

A *MONA LISA* MUCH SOUGHT AFTER

Leonardo showed the Cardinal his last three masterpieces: *Saint Anne* and *Saint John the Baptist* from the Louvre are readily identifiable, and there is no doubt that the third painting was indeed the *Mona Lisa*. But it is interesting to note that Leonardo said that he had painted it for Guiliano de' Medici and not for Francesco del Giocondo!

Guiliano de' Medici was Leonardo's patron from 1513 to 1516. Leonardo did, in fact, live in Rome as part of his household. But if the *Mona Lisa* was painted for Guiliano, then the sitter could not have been Lisa. This is the view held by some who believe that the Louvre painting is a portrait of another woman. They believe that it could be Isabella Gualanda, Pacifica Brandani, or Philiberta of Savoy, all of whom knew Guiliano de' Medici.

But the truth is really quite simple: *Mona Lisa* is indeed Lisa del Giocondo. The proof is provided by her surname and the accounts by Agostino Vespucci and Vasari. Everything makes perfect sense. Indeed, as Leonardo painted very slowly, his paintings were produced, over the course of his life, for the various people who employed him. The *Mona Lisa* was therefore undoubtedly initially commissioned by Francesco del Giocondo. Subsequently, Guiliano de' Medici naturally wanted to possess the magnificent painting when Leonardo lived in his household. But, ultimately, King Francis I of France gained possession of it, because Leonardo died in France in 1519.

Jean-Auguste-Dominique Ingres, *Leonardo da Vinci Dying in the Arms of Francis I*, 1818, Petit Palais - City of Paris Fine Art Museum, Paris

THE *MONA LISA* REMAINED UNFINISHED

When Leonardo died in 1519, he had still not finished his *Mona Lisa*. If one looks closely at certain details, particularly in the lower part of the landscape, which is red-brown in colour, one can see that the artist has only sketched the forms, which are not clearly defined, particularly in the right-hand part where there are two relatively formless areas of land.

La Gioconda, unfinished section detail

2.
LEONARDO AT WORK: THE CREATION OF THE *MONA LISA*

Leonardo da Vinci was a great inventor.
He spent much of his time conceiving all sorts
of machines and trying to understand how
the world works. But that does not mean that
he did not take an interest in other people's work.
His *Mona Lisa* was, in fact, greatly inspired
by portraits executed by other painters.
He even copied some of their ideas—he improved
them and added his own personal touch.

LEONARDO THE COPIER

In Leonardo's time, the portraits were generally very sober, a bit like the current ID photographs, which require the sitter to remain absolutely still and expressionless, and, above all, not smile. Profile portraits were particularly sought after. But there was also a liking for a new style that originated from northern Europe, more precisely from Flanders. The Flemish created a type of portrait that was between a profile portrait and a front view, called a three-quarter portrait. Leonardo really liked this invention because the three-quarter view—more than any other view—created an impression of movement and life. So he chose this view for his *Mona Lisa*.

Antonio del Pollaiolo, *Profile Portrait of a Young Lady*, c.1465, Gemäldegalerie, Berlin

It was also from the Flemish painters that he borrowed the idea of placing Mona Lisa in a room enclosed by a small wall surmounted by two columns, with an opening onto a landscape in the background. This type of composition can be seen in the *Portrait of Benedetto Portinari*, painted by the great Flemish artist Hans Memling, in 1487.

Hans Memling, *Portrait of Benedetto Portinari*, 1487,
Uffizi Gallery, Florence

The position of Mona Lisa's hands was also not Leonardo's idea: many Flemish painters represented their sitter with the hands joined, placed in the foreground of the painting. The painter Rogier Van der Weyden invariably always did this in his female portraits.

Rogier Van der Weyden, *Portrait of a Woman*, c.1445, Gemäldegalerie, Berlin

LIKE AN OPEN DOOR ...

But Leonardo did not just copy other artists' ideas. In the paintings by other artists, there does not seem to be any reason why the figures are depicted in this posture, whereas everything in the *Mona Lisa* is very natural. It is as if one has just opened the door of Mona Lisa's house. The viewer discovers her seated in the loggia, where she is probably admiring the view of the mountains. Since she has heard us entering, she turns towards us. Her right hand has just been placed over the left hand, her body is in three-quarter view, and her face is almost facing the viewer. That is why she is smiling: it is a sign of welcome.

HER GAZE FOLLOWS THE VIEWER EVERYWHERE

Leonardo wanted to depict Lisa in a way that made her as real and alive as possible. That is why he chose a wooden panel that was large enough to produce a life-size portrait of her. As will be seen in greater detail in the following pages, he used a painting technique that involved minute rendering of detail, creating the impression that the facial expression changes slightly—that the Mona Lisa is actually breathing.

The impression that she is alive is so strong that it is often said that it is the only painting in which the model's gaze can follow us, wherever we are in the room. That is why some visitors move from left to right in front of the painting to verify that Mona Lisa is still watching them. And it is true—her gaze follows the viewer. But in actual fact, it is not the only painting in which this phenomenon occurs: when an artist has represented a model's gaze directed at the viewer, it always creates this effect. One only has to look at other paintings in the *Gioconda* room, in which the model's gaze is directed at the viewer: you will see that their gaze also follows the viewer.

SIT UPRIGHT!

Leonardo wanted to represent Lisa in a very natural posture, but at the same time he managed to portray her in a way that was worthy of the women of her time. It is just like when we have our photo taken: we try to be as natural as possible while arranging ourselves to our best advantage. And that is exactly what Lisa did: she is not leisurely sitting back on her chair, but is sitting upright to create an impression of height. With one hand placed over the other, she appears calm, reserved, and very gentle. This is how Florentine bourgeois ladies liked to be represented. The same pose can, for example, be seen in a fresco by a contemporary artist, Domenico Ghirlandaio.

Domenico Ghirlandaio, *The Birth of Saint John the Baptist*, c.1485–1490, church of Santa Maria Novella, Florence

SMILE!

Lisa therefore has the dignified and reserved demeanour of a woman with a high social status, but without the distant—even haughty—expression that can be seen in the traditional portraits of her time, such as in those by Ghirlandaio. On the contrary, Leonardo asked her to wear a charming smile. It is not an expression of laughter, but rather the beginning of a smile. Look closely: the corners of her mouth are barely raised and there is only slight creasing around the eyes.

This famous smile has always fascinated *Mona Lisa*'s fans. It is important to note that a smile is the most complex expression on the human face. A smile can say everything. We smile when we are happy and also when we are having fun, or when we are mocking someone. We also smile when we want to make contact with someone.

As we have already seen, Vasari wrote in his account that Leonardo employed musicians, singers, and clowns to entertain Lisa, to ensure that she always wore a smile on her face. We do not know if this is true, but in any case, her smile certainly enhanced the beauty of her face.

We also smile when someone takes a photo of us!

A ROOM WITH A VIEW

A vast landscape stretches out behind Lisa. On the right, can be seen a river—spanned by a bridge—, which follows its course until it reaches a lake at the foot of high mountains. On the left, a winding path disappears into the mountain tops, behind which is another fairly large river that also flows at the foot of the high mountains.

This landscape has sometimes amazed people. At first sight, there is, in fact, something strange about it: the horizon has not been placed at the same height on either side of the face. It is much higher on the right than it is on the left. That is the

inconsistency. How could Leonardo, who had a very scientific mind, make such a mistake? It is impossible; it is therefore thought that he did this deliberately, perhaps to indicate that the painting contained a secret ...

But let us take a look at a copy of the *Mona Lisa,* which is in the Prado Museum and which we will examine later*... On the far left, can be seen the line of the waterway that is perfectly in line with the waterway on the right. Let us take another look at the *Mona Lisa* in the Louvre: the small waterway can also be seen on the left, but it is much less visible because of the layers of yellow varnish, which we will address later. The *Mona Lisa's* landscape is therefore entirely consistent. The horizon is indeed at the same height on either side of the face.

Leonardo was particularly interested in mountains, which he very often represented in the background of his paintings. In this painting, he created magnificent scenery composed of mountain summits and large lakes—which are very impressive and a little mysterious—behind Mona Lisa.

* See page 45.

3.
A CLOSE LOOK AT THE *MONA LISA*

To gain a better understanding of the *Mona Lisa*, it is important to know something about the painting's condition. The painting is over five hundred years old and, over the course of its long life, it has changed considerably.

THE *MONA LISA* IS NOT A CANVAS!

To begin with, let us talk about the painting's 'framework'—the support on which the painting was painted. All too often it is said that the *Mona Lisa* is a master canvas. Leonardo was, of course, a great master, but the word 'canvas' is not correct. It is true that the word 'canvas' tends to refer to any type of painting, but it is better to be more specific and say that the *Mona Lisa* is a panel. Leonardo chose a very fine poplar panel as a support for his painting; this type of wood was frequently used by painters in Italy.

LA GIOCONDA IS LARGE!

Another belief is that *La Gioconda* is very small, which is entirely incorrect! Obviously, in the vast room in which the painting hangs, surrounded by enormous pictures such as Veronese's *The Wedding at Cana*, *La Gioconda* looks minuscule. However, when it was painted, it was one of the largest portraits of its time. Leonardo wanted a support that would be large enough to represent a life-size version of Lisa, while at that time painted portraits were usually much smaller. So he used a wooden panel measuring 79 centimetres high by 53 wide. He also made sure the panel was very thin and well made.

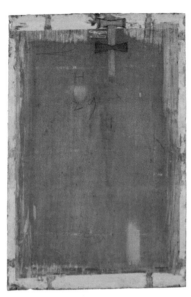

La Gioconda, back of the painting

Leonardo was a great perfectionist and wanted to ensure his masterpiece would stay in good condition for a long time.

Unfortunately, over time, the beautiful poplar wood panel became slightly deformed: the wood, which is easily affected by humidity, has become curved and even slightly cracked. A large crack runs from the upper area of the panel down to Lisa's hair, but stops, almost miraculously, just above her forehead. To prevent this alarming slit, which could cut Lisa's face in two, from further developing, the restorers glued on the back of the painting, pieces of canvas and small pieces of wood, known as butterflies because of their shape.

All these movements of the wood, which was, nevertheless, contained in a frame, have also created an immense network of fine cracks over the entire painted surface. These very fine cracks are particularly visible on the face, giving Mona Lisa rather curious wrinkles.

Raphael, *Portrait of a young woman*, c.1504–1506,
Louvre Museum, Paris

MONA LISA'S BEARD

It is sometimes said that the sides of *La Gioconda* were trimmed. This is based on a copy drawn by one of Leonardo's admirers—the young Raphael—, in which larger columns are represented on either side. There are even several ancient copies of *La Gioconda* that represent the same large columns*. Yet, *La Gioconda* has never been trimmed. The proof lies in her fine beard! Take a close look at the edges of the wood panel: they have never been painted. This is because when Leonardo began his painting, he inserted the panel in a chassis

* See page 53.

(a sort of frame) that enabled him to handle the work without touching the paint. When the paint was applied, it collected near the chassis, and this is what is known as the painting's 'beard'. The presence of this beard proves that the painting has never been trimmed.

Raphael and the other copyists must therefore have been inspired by another version, perhaps a preparatory drawing executed by Leonardo, in which the small columns were more evident.

MONA LISA IN A SMOKY HAZE

Before starting his painting, Leonardo probably executed a large drawing of his composition that enabled him to set out the portrait's main lines on the wooden panel. The paint was, of course, not applied directly to the wood, whose surface was too irregular. Firstly, the panel had to be covered with a preparatory layer that formed an extremely smooth surface that absorbed the paint applied to it. Once the preparatory layer was applied and the outline of La Gioconda drawn with a pencil, the colours could finally be painted on the surface.

These colours were made from pigments—coloured materials that were ground and mixed with a binder. These pigments were commonplace and frequently used in those days. For Lisa's skin, the artist applied lead white coloured with vermillion to create pink. The shadows were rendered with earth colours. The blue used for the landscape was created using lapis lazuli, a semi-precious stone that was very expensive and which is still used today for jewellery!

ISN'T IT A BIT
SFUMATO?

So, Leonardo was doing nothing new with these pigments. Rather, his genius lies in the way he used them. He used oil as a binder, which enabled him to paint very thin and transparent layers of colour, known as glazes. And there are no visible brushstrokes! Everything was done in a very subtle and meticulous way. Look at how the shadows merge into the light in the landscape and the face, around the eyes and the mouth: there are no lines ...

Everything is extremely soft, as though seen through a thin veil of fog or smoke. This effect is known as *sfumato*. This is an Italian word that means 'smoky'. Leonardo painted *La Gioconda* as though she appears through a light mist. Based on this technique, nothing is rigid and if anything, the painting appears to vibrate! This is how, thanks to *sfumato*, he succeeded in bringing the face to life thus giving *Mona Lisa* a truly lifelike quality.

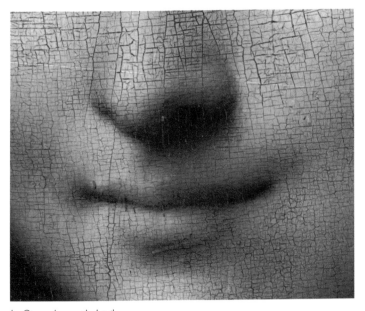

La Gioconda, mouth detail

LA GIOCONDA IS WELL AND TRULY VARNISHED!

Once the painting was completed, a layer of varnish was often applied to the surface to protect the paint. However Leonardo never finished his picture, which was varnished after his death. Over time, this varnish yellowed and became dirty. So, to clean it up a new layer of varnish was applied. However, as the years passed these layers of varnish became very thick and increasingly yellow. There are several layers of old varnish over *La Gioconda* and this acts like a thick yellow filter that transforms and affects all the colours. It is like looking at the painting with glasses with yellow lenses! The shadows are darker, the blues have been made greener, and the whites have become yellow. This is why *La Gioconda* does not have the healthiest of complexions and why the sky looks polluted. Under the layers of varnish, the colours are very different: the face and hands have white and pink hues and the sky and water are brighter shades of blue. To see these true colours under the old layers of varnish, the painting was examined in a laboratory.

THE INFRARED IMAGE OF *LA GIOCONDA*

As with human beings, works of art can be examined in a laboratory to assess their condition. They are photographed with different rays (ultraviolet, infrared, and X-rays) to see what lies under their 'skin'. Using radiography, Mona Lisa seems to disappear! Leonardo painted her with so little paint that the X-rays almost pass right through her. However, using infrared

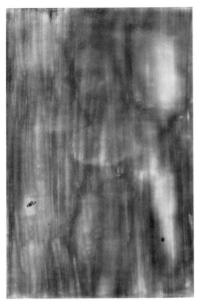

La Gioconda, radiography   *La Gioconda*, infrared reflectography

she is revealed even more clearly. If you examine a standard photograph and the infrared image, it becomes easier to understand the composition painted by Leonardo.

This reveals that Mona Lisa is sitting on a round-back seat: you can see the armrest and the supporting balusters. In Italy, this is known as a *sedile a pozzetto*. This armchair is not facing the viewer but rather seen from the side, in a room with a slighty illuminated floor, enclosed at the end by a small balustrade on which stand two small columns.

La Gioconda's clothing is also more clearly visible in the infrared image because all the transparency of the veils is revealed. Lisa is wearing a dress covered by a large silk veil known as a *guarnello*, attached at the bosom with embroidered gold

Armchair a *pozzetto*, 16th century

thread creating an interlacing geometric motif. This veil is slightly pulled up over her right elbow and on the other side, she has raised it over her left shoulder to create a sort of scarf and enhance her elegance. All these transparent veils have become darker because of the layers of varnish and make Mona Lisa look fatter than she really is. In fact, she is actually quite slim, which is no surprise because, circa 1503, she was twenty-four years old. It is also evident that the sleeves of her garment are independent: they are fastened to the dress at the shoulders and here you can see a beautiful white blouse that Lisa is wearing underneath. A very fine veil covers her head. Her hair is not as undone as it seems. Only a few locks at the front are loose on the sides of the face, but the rest is held in place with a hairpiece, whose shape is clearly visible on the infrared image.

This very dark appearance has led some to claim that Lisa is dressed very simply and perhaps in mourning attire. However, in reality, even though she is wearing no jewellery, her attire is very rich and sophisticated, and was more colourful than it now appears. This is no surprise because Lisa was a rich woman and most importantly, she was the wife of a silk merchant. That is why she has all these silk veils!

La Gioconda, detail of the interlacing embroidery motif of the dress

A TWIN SISTER

All the details of the picture can also be seen in a recently restored copy of *La Gioconda* held in the Museo del Prado. In this work, Mona Lisa's garment is slightly green; the sleeves are orange-red and everything is covered with transparent silk veils. The landscape is dominated by different shades of blue.

This picture was painted by one of Leonardo's pupils while he was working. But the pupil must have finished his picture before the master, because he did not copy some of the details that Leonardo added at the end, such as the small end of the armrest that is visible in the Prado *Gioconda*, but which Leonardo eventually covered with a veil in his work.

Leonardo da Vinci's pupil, *La Gioconda*, c.1508–1516, Prado Museum, Madrid

4.

THE 'MYSTERIES' OF *LA GIOCONDA*

It is often said that Mona Lisa has a secret.
This is the mystery of *La Gioconda*—this is why
many people look at her and try to work out
why she is smiling or look for hidden forms
and messages in the painting.
But did Leonardo really hide a secret
in his painting?

ARE THERE HIDDEN SIGNS IN THE PICTURE?

Leonardo da Vinci was fascinated by geometry and mathematics. When you closely observe *La Gioconda*, you realise that the construction of its composition is highly organised: he placed Lisa's left eye right in the centre of the width of the picture; so the face is quite naturally in the middle of the painting. He gave the face a very regular and harmonious shape, which suggests a geometric construction. Some people believe that

La Gioconda, detail of the face and landscape in the background

Leonardo may have concealed a message via a combination of geometric forms, but they have never discovered anything! Likewise, researchers have analysed the details in the landscape, such as the winding road on the left and the small bride on the right, but again, no one has discovered any hidden messages.

Some people also claim to have found letters, numbers, and shapes hidden in the painting; in fact, they were mistaken by the cracks in the painted surface and the layers of yellowed varnish that have formed curious shapes that Leonardo never intended to create.

So, no one has ever really proved that there is a shape or a message concealed in *La Gioconda*—probably because it does not exist!

WHY IS SHE SMILING?

This is a common question. As we have already said, it was probably to highlight her beauty, as we do when someone takes a photo of us. Maybe she is smiling because she saw something funny that amused her or made her happy. Obviously, people are curious about what could have made her smile in this way. It is as though Lisa has been captured at a particular moment in her life. It seems as though something is going on, but we do not know exactly what!

WAS LISA PREGNANT?

Some people have suggested that Lisa is smiling because she was pregnant. The large veil that covers her dress—the *guarnello*, which we have already mentioned—is a garment that can be seen on other portraits of Renaissance women, and particularly in a portrait by Sandro Botticelli in which the woman is pregnant. So, could this *guarnello* indicate that Lisa was also pregnant? If that were true, *La Gioconda* would have been commissioned at the beginning of 1502, just when Lisa was expecting Andrea, who was born in December. Unfortunately, it is difficult to defend this theory, because, while in Botticelli's work the lady's pregnant condition is clearly visible, in Leonardo's painting it is not evident, and Lisa is slim.

Sandro Botticelli, *Portrait of a Woman*, 1470–1480, The Victoria and Albert Museum, London

'MRS HAPPY' IS ALWAYS SMILING

The smile was also perhaps a play on words, because 'Giocondo', the family name, means 'happy' in Italian. So, what better way to represent the wife of Mr Happy than with a wonderful smile! This is probably why she was soon called 'La Gioconda': it obviously referred to 'Mr Happy's wife' and also meant 'the happy woman'.

EVERYONE SEES *LA GIOCONDA* DIFFERENTLY

We also feel that *La Gioconda* is trying to tell us something with her smile. Because this smile is for the viewer—*she* is looking at *us*! Of course, it is a very welcoming smile, and one feels that she is about to say something to us, like: 'please, come in'. Leonardo succeeded in creating a portrait that communicates with the viewer. Maybe this is *La Gioconda's* real secret: a picture that is capable of creating an emotional bond between people whose lives are separated by centuries. This is the magic and poetry of painting and this is what gives us such pleasure when we look at paintings. As she smiles at us, *La Gioconda* is asking us many questions, but without giving us the answers. It is up to us to use our imagination and dream with her. It is up to each individual to imagine the secret that lies behind Mona Lisa's smile.

5.

THE MOST FAMOUS PAINTING IN THE WORLD

Ever since it was painted, *La Gioconda* has been a source of fascination. No one had ever seen a painting that imitated reality so convincingly. And no one had ever seen a portrait that seemed so alive, as though the sitter were breathing! La Gioconda became an instant legend. In Vasari's words: 'It was a thing more divine than human to behold, and it was held to be something marvellous, in that it was not other than alive'.

A little later, in 1625, Cassiano dal Pozzo, whom we have already mentioned, gazed at the portrait in wonder and declared that it was the 'finest portrait in the kingdom' of France! In Louis XIV's day, the masterpiece was held in the Château of Versailles in the King's own apartment, indicating that it has always been seen as one of the most precious treasures.

1001 COPIES OF *LA GIOCONDA*

La Gioconda was in fact widely copied at this time. Every art lover wanted to have their own Gioconda in their house. Today, we know of one hundred and fifty ancient copies of the Louvre picture! And copies are still being created. Nowadays, though, art lovers are often happy to settle for a poster or a postcard.

Since it was placed in the Louvre Museum in 1797, it has always been given a place of honour amongst the great masterpieces of painting. Today, it hangs in the State Room, also known as the Gioconda Room, which is one of the largest rooms in the Louvre.

Copy of Leonardo da Vinci, *La Gioconda*, 17th century, Museum of Ancient and Contemporary Art, Epinal

THE THEFT OF *LA GIOCONDA*

La Gioconda's fame spread around the world after an incredible event. On 21 August 1911, a certain Vincenzo Peruggia, who was working at the Louvre as a building painter, took the painting off the wall, removed its frame, and stole it without being spotted. The museum guards only noticed it was missing several hours later and it caused a scandal! The disappearance of the painting was reported all around the world.

September 1911, the theft of *La Gioconda* at the Louvre

Its photograph was printed on every newspaper at the time. It became the most sought after and most famous painting in the world.

It was not until 1913 that the painting was finally retrieved. Vincenzo Peruggia had taken it to Italy and offered it to the famous Uffizi Gallery in Florence. When the Uffizi curators realised that it was the real *Gioconda*, they had him arrested and retrieved the painting, which they then returned to France.

THE MOST PROTECTED PAINTING
IN THE WORLD

Ever since, the Musée du Louvre has kept *La Gioconda* like a precious treasure. Henceforth, like any other celebrity, she is under strict surveillance. During the two World Wars, it was evacuated to safe and secret locations. It was transported in a luxurious crate and its condition was checked regularly.

At the time, in the museum, glass was inserted inside its frame to protect it from visitors going too near to it. Unfortunately, to no avail, because in 1956, a madman threw a large stone at the painting, breaking the glass and damaging the *Mona Lisa's* left elbow: this is the only really damaged part of the painting. Since 1974, the painting has been housed in a large air-conditioned glass case that maintains its condition and most importantly, protects it from the crowds that flock to see it. In 2005, it was placed on its own on a large picture rail in the State Room. It is now high enough for everyone to see. But, at the same time, one can no longer really go up to it and see it close up. But this protection is indispensable! Since its new installation in 2005, it has been attacked several times, particularly in 2009 when a deranged woman threw a cup of coffee over the picture—but this time, the *Mona Lisa* was completely safe because the glass case is extremely tough!

A MODEL FOR ARTISTS

After the incredible theft of *La Gioconda*, artists began to experiment with her image. Marcel Duchamp gave her a moustache, Fernand Léger pasted her next to a bunch of keys and a tin of sardines, Andy Warhol created multiple images of her in every colour, and Fernando Botero made her fat.

L. H. O. O. Q.

Marcel Duchamp, *LHOOQ*, 1919, National Museum of Modern Art – Centre Georges-Pompidou, Paris

Fernand Léger, *La Gioconda with Keys*, 1930,
Fernand Léger Museum, Biot

Andy Warhol, *Thirty Are Better Than One*, 1963,
private collection

Fernando Botero, *Mona Lisa*, 1978, Botero Museum,
Bogota

Yan Pei-Ming, *Mona Lisa's Funeral* (detail of the polyptych, oil on canvas), 2008
Louvre Abu Dhabi, Abu Dhabi

More recently, the Chinese painter Yan Pei-Ming painted a large *Gioconda* in black and white, which gave her a sadder appearance. These are just a few examples of the many ways in which *La Gioconda* has been represented by artists over the years.

THE MOST WIDELY REPRODUCED IMAGE IN THE WORLD

La Gioconda also turns up everywhere in our daily lives: in films, comics, advertisements, on book covers, on the outsides of pizzerias ... her image is used all round the world. It is true that her gaze and smile make her instantly recognisable. This is why many politicians adopt the same pose as *La Gioconda* for their portraits.

HELLO MONA LISA!

La Gioconda is so famous that some people even think she really exists. Now and again, she receives letters at the Louvre: people wishing her a happy birthday or a Merry Christmas and even asking her if she is in good health!

CREDITS

Photo credits

For Adèle, Alice, Élise, Hector,
Louise, Oreste, Théophile, and Thomas.

Éditions du musée du Louvre
Chief editor: Violaine Bouvet-Lanselle
Editorial coordination: Catherine Dupont and Camille Sourisse
Iconography: Camille Sourisse
© Musée du Louvre, 2017 – ISBN 978-2-35031-564-5

Éditions Actes Sud
Editor: Isabelle Péhourticq assisted by Fanny Gauvin and Camille Giordani-Caffet
Creative director: Kamy Pakdel
Artistic director: Guillaume Berga
© Actes Sud, 2017 – ISBN 978-2-330-07323-7

In compliance with act 49.956 of 16 July 1949 relating to publications for young people.
Reproduced and printed in October 2018 by Pbtisk printworks in Czech Republic
for Éditions ACTES SUD,
Le Méjan, Place Nina-Berberova, 13200 Arles.
1st edition: January 2017